Learning to Stand Against the Attacks of Satan

*Your Greatest Arsenal is the
True Word of God*

Kenneth D. Reed, Sr.

WESTBOW
PRESS
A DIVISION OF THOMAS NELSON

Cover Photography – Angelica Expressions

WestBow Press books may be ordered through booksellers or by contacting:

WestBow Press
A Division of Thomas Nelson
1663 Liberty Drive
Bloomington, IN 47403
www.westbowpress.com
1-(866) 928-1240

ISBN: 978-1-4497-4280-5 (sc)
ISBN: 978-1-4497-4281-2 (e)

Library of Congress Control Number: 2012904355

Printed in the United States of America

WestBow Press rev. date: 08/29/2012

Dedication

THIS BOOK IS DEDICATED TO my parents Arthur and Eartha Reed whom not only taught me the ways of holiness but were true examples. I love you Mom and Dad, and I will see you again.

Acknowledgements

My wife of 21 years of marriage, Ann Marie, thank you for your prayers, for your encouragement, for being by my side in life and ministry, but most of all thank you for always believing in me. I love you. My children Ken Jr., William, and Diamond, who taught me how to not just be a Dad, but also how to be a real Father. You guys make me so proud and I love you with all of my heart.

My siblings Margie, Betty, Lois, Netra, Dorothy, Michael, Ricky, Jerry, Bobby, Milton, and Arthur, thank you for taking care of your baby brother, love you all. I would like to acknowledge Pastor C. James Starks, Pastor Anthony Starks, Pastor Michael Reed, and special thanks to Bishop Edgar L. Vann for your covering, your prayers, and for encouraging me to be a *"Winning Pastor"*

I would also like to acknowledge the Divine Favor Ministries Church family, who inspired me to reach my full potential and write this book, love you DFMites. I would also like to thank my awesome staff, Tamar Butler, Brice Evans, Dionne Hill, Elthel Schroeder, and Mary Wells. Thank you for your hard work, support, and dedication.

Table of Contents

Preface

SATAN HAS CAUSED SOME BELIEVERS to lower their standards and to place limitations on life by influencing them to think, *"My life will never get any better."* This book was written to be your weapon of resources to Learn to stand against the Attacks of Satan.

> *"The thief cometh not, but for to steal, and to kill, and to destroy: I am come that they might have life, and that they might have it more abundantly."*
> John 10:10

The word *"abundance"* means overflowing, and whenever Satan knows that God has a blessing for you, he will attack and try to stop the blessings that are coming your way because he doesn't want to see you living in abundance and walking upright with the Lord, so he comes to steal your riches, kill your inheritance, and to destroy your faith in God, but remember that your greatest arsenal is to stand on the true word of God.

Chapter 1

"Learning the Tactics of Satan's Attacks"

JESUS PREPARED HIS DISCIPLES FOR everything, including war. They saw him cast out demons, in fact, He sent them out to do the same. However, before He sent them out, He charged them to become as the Bible says in Matthew 10:16 *"wise as serpents yet innocent and harmless as doves."*

This combination of divine wisdom and Christ-like innocence is the source of all spiritual victory, but we must learn the ways of God, which means we must think with wisdom, and we must be pure of heart that we may see God and gain discernment.

Remember Adam and Eve were in paradise when they fell. Solomon wrote three books of Scripture, and he actually gazed upon the glory of God, yet he fell, and let us not forget Lucifer himself was once in heaven pouring out praise to God. Yes, we have all seen many who have fallen and Jesus also warned in Matthew 24:12 *"And because iniquity shall abound, the love of many shall wax cold."*

Satan has been deceiving mankind for thousands of years, so that means we have to be bold in our prayer life. I know many well-meaning Christians have approached the field of battle with laid-back attitudes and have suffered greatly for it. Satan is out to deceive us; he is out to torment and destroy us. He wants to keep us from the truth because he knows that the true Word of God, when it is applied to our lives, it will set us free.

The Mind Game

WHAT IS SATAN'S REAL STRATEGY in his attacks? The attacks of Satan start in the mind. The mind is his primary approach of establishing destruction in our lives and few Christians realize this important fact. In 2 Corinthians 10:4, the Bible speaks of the *"weapons of our warfare"* and it's important to realize that we are at war and when I speak of war, I am speaking of life and death, a fight for our very spiritual lives, so we must come to the realization that we need to fight if we are to survive. Where does this war begin? It begins in the mind. The area of our thoughts is the main battleground. The warfare starts in the mind, but then if allowed; it will spread to other areas of our lives as well.

> 2 Corinthians 10:5
> *"Casting down imaginations, and every high thing that exalteth itself against the knowledge of God, and bringing into captivity every thought to the obedience of Christ."*

This verse speaks of *"casting down imaginations."* The word *"imaginations"* translated in the Greek, actually means: *"a reasoning or decision."* This speaks of the way we so often are able to take the plain truth of God's word and twist it in such a way that it's no longer absolute. It turns in such a way that our specific situation is so special or unique that we are not bound by the same rules as everyone else. We downsize; we make excuses, and reason the truth into exactly what we want to hear, but Paul is saying we are to use our spiritual weapons to break down these arguments that go on in our minds put there by the snake, Satan himself.

Once again, the battleground is in the mind, and thoughts are what Satan wants to slip in there. It is so often just one little thought placed in our minds by Satan himself that will make us say and do things that are so destructive and hurtful to people and to the body of Christ. You see; the enemy's primary approach is to drop a THOUGHT into our minds. He wants us to accept it and then act upon it, and the danger is that once we do, that thought can become a stronghold. A stronghold is anything that exalts itself in our minds pretending to be bigger or more powerful than our God. Satan's lying thoughts can really have a stronghold on people! Thoughts can hold you like a vise and keep you from the truth. One lie and Satan can hold you in a place of sickness, suffering, torment, bitterness, and unforgiveness, and it will last just as long as you permit it and as long as you accept it! Many of us are held captive by a thought, and that thought brings fear.

The devil can bring thousands of thoughts to our minds. These thoughts bring fear, and when they take root in our mind, we begin to speak them and what was once an accusing voice now becomes your voice saying, "I'm no good, God can't use me" and so on. This is nothing more than a crafty but deadly trick of the enemy. So don't fall into his trap. Paul says we need to bring every thought into the truth of God's Word! Paul was speaking this as he was undergoing a difficult trial personally. Paul's credibility was called into question, and his response may seem weak but he fights his battles by using God's mighty weapons, not men. He says these weapons are the only ones that will tear down the strongholds of the enemy. These are the only weapons that will ensure spiritual victory. This is the only way to overcome the devil by using the Word of God! John 8:44 *"When he speaketh a lie, he speaketh of his own: for he is a liar, and the father of it."* Remember, the devil is not only a liar; he is the father of all lies! He can't tell the truth, and he wants to convince you that your life is messed up and can't be fixed, but understand the devil wants you to suffer; he wants to rob you of your joy; he wants to rob you of your peace, your family, and your relationships, because he comes to steal, kill and destroy!

Paul says the weapons that are available to us are mighty through God not just to get by, but to demolish these strongholds, so we must put our faith into action and act on the Word of God! When the enemy comes in with these thoughts and try to torment us or cause us to live and act contrary to the Word of God, we need to begin to fight with the same weapons Jesus used to defeat Satan. All Jesus did was quote the Word of God with faith and assurance. No Christian can expect to be victorious in spiritual warfare that has not become proficient with the sword of the spirit which is the word of God. Your word and my word have no authority at all over Satan's kingdom; it is only God's word that lives in your heart coming out of your mouth that breaks Satan's power.

The Bible says in St. Matthew 4:4 *"Man shall not live by bread alone, but by every word that proceedeth out of the mouth of God."*

This is the plan Jesus used when he thrashed the devil. Satan placed the thought. In St. Matthew 4:3, Satan challenged Jesus to *"Turn these stones to bread."* However, Jesus rejected that thought and replaced it with one of God's thoughts by saying *"It is written!"* St. Matthew 4:7 *"Thou shalt not temp the Lord, thy God."* You can beat the devil every time by saying, *"It is written!"*

When the enemy tells you, *"You don't have anything, look at what this one got, and look at what that one got"*, replace that thought with *"It is written!"*

Philippians 4:19
"But my God shall supply all your need according to his riches in glory by Christ Jesus."

When the Satan causes you to shed tears of sadness, replace that thought with *"It is written! Psalms 30:5 "Weeping may endure for the night, but joy comes in the morning"*

When Satan tells you, *"you can't make it, you can't do, you can't get any help"* replace that thought with *"It is written!"*

Philippians 4:13
"I can do all things though Christ that strengthens me"

When Satan tells you, *"you have troub with your life, trouble with your spouse, trouble with your children, trouble at church"* replace that thought with "It is written!

St. John 14:1-3
"Let not your heart be troubled: ye believe in God, believe also in me. In my Father's house are many mansions: if it were not so, I would have told you. I go to prepare a place for you. And if I go and prepare a place for you, I will come again, and receive you unto myself; that where I am, there ye may be also."

Remember Satan seeks to attack the mind because he realizes that all actions start with a thought. That is why it is imperative that we read, study, and know the word of God for ourselves and when (not if) Satan starts his attacks, the Holy Spirit will bring your teaching back to your remembrance.

John 14:26
"But the Comforter, which is the Holy Ghost, whom the Father will send in my name, he shall teach you all things, and bring all things to your remembrance, whatsoever I have said unto you."

Chapter 2

"Learning to Protect Heart Against the Attacks of Satan"

THE HUMAN HEART IS A muscular organ that provides a continuous circulation of blood through the body. The heart is one of the most vital parts of the human body, for without the heart the body cannot be kept alive. The heart is considered the center of our emotions, our feelings, our intellect, and it is also associated with our will. The heart has a lot to do with who we are and what we are and more significantly it describes our relationship with God.

The *"heart"* is not just the physical organ pumping blood through the body, but the heart is also the *"soul"* and just as the body is lifeless without the heart, so is it spiritually. The term *"Spiritual Warfare"* is taught because the things that we fight against are of a spiritual nature.

Ephesians 6:12
"For we wrestle not against flesh and blood, but against principalities, against powers, against the rulers of the

darkness of this world, against spiritual wickedness in high places."

Spiritual warfare is the trials and tribulations that come into our lives which cause faith to be released and it demonstrates the power of God to the world. It also causes the Christian to mature spiritually by becoming more rooted and grounded in God. To achieve this, we have to protect our hearts, not just because it is vital to living and having life, but because it is vital to having life more abundantly the way God says we should.

The reason so many believers are being defeated is because they do not recognize the weapons that the enemy uses, and if you don't understand the tactics of Satan, you will not be able to fight effectively. Satan knows that the doorway to your desires is through your heart. And in Spiritual battle, there will be times when Satan tries to attack our hearts. Jesus said in Proverbs 4:23, *"...with all diligence guard your heart"* that means the heart should receive the greatest effort and it has to be protected!

The word of God says in Proverbs 4:24 *"Put away from thee a froward mouth, and perverse lips put far from thee."* For example, gossip, criticism, dirty jokes, words that hurt, and words that divide come from a forward mouth. A *"Forward Mouth"* is words of ill nature. In other words, it's saying, put away from thee *"a deceitful mouth, a lying mouth, and a dishonest mouth."*

Protecting your heart means you must also keep your mouth right. God informs us in Matthew 12:34 *"O generation of vipers, how can ye, being evil, speak good things? For out of the abundance of the heart the mouth speaketh."*

The word of God is saying according to the scripture, *"a wrong mouth and a right heart will not dwell in the same body."* Another thing that we as people of God need to know is that, *"there is power in the words you speak."*

Proverbs 18:21
"Death and Life are in the power of the tongue."

Sometimes it's not Satan that causes destruction in our lives; it's the words we speak into our own lives. In other words, positive words bring positive results, while negative words bring negative results! Satan knows the power of words. When he entered the serpent and tempted Eve, he challenged the word.

Genesis 3:1
"Now the serpent was more subtle than any beast of the field which the LORD God had made. And he said unto the woman, Yea, hath God said, ye shall not eat of every tree of the garden?"

Observe if you, will the path by which Satan used to get to the *"heart"* of Eve. Satan used words. He simply spoke to her. Satan spoke and Eve listened to what he had to say. So what that tells me is we have to be very careful who we listen to because one of the main weapons that Satan will use to fight against you is your ears. Because He knows your ears are speedy access to your heart. He knows if someone can tell you something in your ear and cause you to believe it in your mind, in matter of time, what was spoken into your ears contaminates your heart. Satan spoke words in Eve's ear; she listened to what he had to say, and after listening to what he had to say, she began to speak back to Satan.

Genesis 3:2
"And the woman said unto the serpent, We may eat of the fruit of the trees of the garden:

Observe once again how Eve began to communicate with Satan, and after that, it was only a matter of time before what was spoken into her ears contaminated her heart. For that very reason the word of God warns us that we cannot communicate with just anybody.

1st Corinthians 15:33
"Be not deceived: evil communication corrupt good manners"

People of God, *(1) you have to be careful who you talk to, and (2) you also have to be careful who you listen to.* We cannot communicate with everybody. You must understand that the wrong people will talk you out of your miracle, chat you out of your healing, and whisper you out of your blessing. As a matter of fact, you can't even afford to have negative people around you, because when you need a miracle or a breakthrough, you need to have the right people around you. In other words, you have to create an environment for faith to grow and develop, and negativity will kill the Spirit of Faith.

When you let down your defenses and listen to the words that Satan speaks into your ears and also carry on a conversation with him, the consequence can and will be deadly. Eve allowed the wrong person to speak into her life. Remember, anything that is contrary to the word of God is a lie. And Satan is the father of lies.

John 8:44
"When he speaketh a lie, he speaketh of his own: for he is a liar and the father of it."

When Eve listened to the words of Satan, it caused her to speak back to him, and when they began to be conversant, she opened up her *"heart"* to him, and when she opened up her *"heart"* to him, he could contaminate it.

This reminds me of another person that the Bible speaks about in the 16th chapter of Judges, a man by the name of Samson. Samson was blessed by God with great strength, but he fell victim to another serpent named Delilah. Just as Eve did, he listened to the deceptive words that sounded so sweet in his ears. However, what those words did was contaminate his heart. He listened, communicated, and conversant with the enemy, and once that happened, he was no longer dedicated to God, for he exposed the very secret that connected him to God. The Bible warns us to be careful who we talk to because corrupt talk leads to corrupt living!

> 1st Corinthians 15:33
> *"Be not deceived: evil communications corrupt good manners."*

Satan understood the power of words and he challenged the word that God gave to Adam, and just as Satan challenged the word God gave to Adam, surely he is going to challenge the word God gives to you also.

Another way that we can protect our heart is to be careful of what we look at. The word *"look"* means to set one's sight on a particular object. Are you aware of the fact that what your eyes see will affect your heart? That is why we're told in Proverbs 4:25 *"Let thine eyes look right on, and let thine eyelids look straight before thee."*

A vast level of the temptation that you and I face in life is brought on through our eyes. I really believe that if the eyes are controlled, it will eliminate a great deal of the temptation. The Bible says in Psalms 81:12 *"So I gave them up unto their own heart's lust: and they walked in their own counsels."*

The *"Heart's Lust"* originates from the eyes, because what the eyes see, the heart will want. Thus, it's important to keep the eyes focused because when you allow your eyes to run freely without any control, you will contaminate your heart. Did you know that most of your memory is formed by the eyes? It is said you can remember more than 30% of what you see and only about 20% of what you hear. Satan's strategy in the *"Garden of Eden"* was to persuade Eve to look because he knows the eyes are the most influential part of the body.

> Genesis 3:6
> *"And when the woman saw that the tree was good for food, and that it was pleasant to the eyes, and a tree to be desired to make one wise, she took of the fruit thereof, and did eat, and gave also unto her husband with her; and he did eat."*

Satan succeeded in getting her to stare on the forbidden fruit and the longer she looked, the more difficult it was for her to turn her eyes away. Soon she forgot all about God's warning of sure judgment because ALL she could see was the tree and its fruit. I use to hear some men say all the time concerning women *"Awe, I'm just looking"* but I always warn them to be careful, because the longer you look; the more desire grows, and the more difficult it is to turn your eyes away. Soon you'll lose all sense of proportion, forget about your commitment to your spouse, to your children, to your church, and to God, and it all started with, *"Awe; I'm just looking."*

> Job 31:1
> *"I made a covenant with mine eyes, why then should I think upon a maid?"*

My advice to you is to stop looking at your problems, stop looking at your situations, stop looking at your circumstances and *"let thine eyelids look straight!*

You can also protect your heart against the attacks of Satan by allowing your steps to be ordered by the Lord. Did you know that where your feet trod will cause a heart's response? It's not a good idea to just turn your feet loose to go anywhere they want to go. The Bible says in Proverbs 4:26, *"Ponder the path of, thy feet, and let all thy ways be established."* The word *"Ponder"* means to weigh mentally or to think deeply about. We should use wisdom in choosing our path of life. To achieve this, we should have a "Planned Walk."

The advice that I usually give to the young adults at DFM is before you buy that new house, that new car, and even before you say the words, *"I do,"* before you make any major decisions in life, ponder over it first. Take your time and pray about it, and ask God to order your steps. Amos warns us to be careful who you walk with.

Amos 3:3
"Can two walk together, except they are agreed?

Everybody is not walking in the same direction, you're walking in. They may be walking the same way, but not in the same direction. We need a protected walk. The word of God also says in Psalm 37:23 *"The steps of a good man are ordered by the Lord."* This means that if I am walking in the favor of God and my steps are ordered by the Lord, then every place I set my foot, he will give me the victory and the walls of Jericho in my life must come tumbling down. When you allow the Lord to order your steps, you will have the favor of God in your life.

Control the Entryways

THE BEST WAY TO PROTECT your heart is to control what you allow to pass through these entryways. Your ears, who are you listening to? Your mouth, who are you communicating with? Your eyes, what are you looking at? Your feet, are your steps ordered by the Lord? Remember if your heart is not right, then the rest of you will not be either.

Chapter 3

"Learning to Stand Against Satan's Attacks of Temptation"

As Christians we are at war with Satan, and one of his biggest artilleries is the weapon of Temptation? It's just like putting bait on a mouse trap and the mouse comes up to take the bait, and it gets caught in the trap. In the same way, Satan sets traps for us also. Just as cheese is placed as bait for a mouse, he places that desired thing as the bait on the trap he has set for you. The word of God says in St. James 1:12 *"Blessed is the man who perseveres under trial, because when he has stood the test, he will receive the crown of life that God has promised to those who love him."*

The person that does not fall to temptation will be happy, and he will be rewarded with a joyful and fulfilling life that can only come from being obedient to God, so the question is *"What do we do to stay out of Satan's trap?"* The first thing; do not be fooled when tempted.

James 1:13
*"When tempted, no one should say, "God is tempting me. For
God cannot be tempted by evil, nor does he tempt anyone."*

Notice it says *"When tempted"* not *"If tempted?"* That means you will
be tempted. In other words, no one is exempt. Don't be fooled into
thinking that Satan will not tempt you. If he tried to tempt Jesus;
he is going to try to tempt you. However, remember the sin is not
being tempted; the sin is yielding to the temptation. If you happen
to get caught in his trap, you can't blame it on others. When you fall
to temptation, you can't blame God, you can't blame your family
or your friends, and you can't even blame the devil, because it's
nobody's fault but yours. All Satan did was put the trap out, and no
one can make you do anything you don't want to do. Stop blaming
others for what you have done.

Another way you can stay out of Satan's trap is not to let your guard
down. Listen to what James says in St. James 1:14 *"but every man is
tempted, when he is drawn away of his own lust, and enticed."*

The first step in Satan's plan to catch you is *"Desire."* The Bible
says that when the lords of the Philistines hired Delilah to find out
where Samson's strength lies, they said to her *"Entice him."* The word
"entice" means to seduce or persuade. Delilah enticed Samson and
she talked to him and found out where his great strength lies. You
see it was more than just sex; she enticed him, then once she enticed
him, he opens up to her, and she finds out what's in his heart, and
she find out his secret. Samson's focus was on the bait and not the
trap and then they were able to overpower him, blind him, and afflict
him, which ultimately lead to his death.

The second step in the Satan's plan to catch you is *"Deception."*
Understand that the devil knows exactly what to send you. In other

words, he knows the right bait to use. How does he know? He has studied you and calculated up the statistics and knows just what to send your way. As a matter of fact, he's been studying you all your life and he knows what it could take to cause you to cross that line. He's not going to bait your trap with spinach if you hate spinach, he going to bait it with something you desire.

The third step in Satan's plan to catch you is *"Disobedience."* St. James 1:15 *"Then, when desire has conceived, it gives birth to sin; and sin, when it is full-grown, brings forth death."* Temptation starts in the mind, but ends up in sin, that leads to the last step in the Satan's plan which is Death. For the Bible warns us in Romans 6:23 *"For the wages of sin is death."* To stay out of Satan's trap, do not focus on the bait because if you keep looking at the bait and wondering about the bait, then you will begin to try to justify taking the bait and the next thing you know, you're caught! We are the first fruits of all God created and instead of focusing on the bait, focus on the Word of God.

I read about men who trap animals in Africa for zoos in America, and it is said that one of the hardest animals to catch is the ring-tailed monkey, but for the Zulus of that continent it's simple. They've been catching this little animal with ease for years. The method the Zulus use is based on knowledge of the animal. Their trap is nothing more than a melon growing on a vine. The seeds of this melon are a favorite of the monkey, knowing this; the Zulus simply cut a hole in the melon, just large enough for the monkey to insert his hand to reach the seeds inside. The monkey will stick his hand in, grab as many seeds as he can, then start to withdraw it; he can't because his fist is now larger than the hole. The monkey will pull and tug, screech and fight the melon for hours, but he can't get free of the trap, unless he gives up the seeds, which he refuses to do. Meanwhile, the Zulus sneak up and nab him, and that is how we get caught too.

We too are being trapped, and we have only two options to give in on temptation or to fight. As long as we are in this body, we will encounter temptation, and we either submit to it or submit to God. We either draw near to the temptation or draw near to God. We either depend on what we can do or depend on what God can do to and through us.

I ran across a site called snopes.com that gave a graphic story on *"How to Kill a Wolf Eskimo Style"*. It stated that when an Eskimo is out hunting wolves, he has a unique method of setting the bait. Wolves are very smart and perceptive. They can literally smell scents that signal danger to them, and to overcome this advantage of the wolf; the Eskimo takes a very sharp knife and dips it in the blood of an animal that will attract the wolf. He allows the blood to dry and dips it again and again to make sure he has a thick layer of blood on the knife. Once he has the layer just right, he freezes the knife with the blood. After the knife is frozen, he takes the knife and buries it blade up in the ground. The wolf smells the blood and seeks it out. When it finds the blood covered knife, it begins to lick the blood off enjoying its taste. What the wolf does not realize (and neither do we) is that the enjoyment is temporary, and it will cost him its life. The wolf continues to lick the blood covered knife not realizing it is actually drinking its own blood, because the knife is slowing cutting into its tongue and mouth as he continues licking, the blood he is drinking is his own. The Eskimo later comes along and picks up the dead wolf. The wolf died because his focus was on the bait and not the trap.

Although we do not always think about it, but Satan is always thinking of ways to *"bait"* us. If you find yourself being baited by Satan, do not give in to the bait. If you are baited spiritually or emotionally, walk away, seek God's escape route that he has already provided for you.

Chapter 4

"Learning to be Cautious of Satan's Attacks of Bearing False Gifts"

SOMETIMES WE AS BELIEVERS HAVE to be very careful of the gifts that we accept from people, especially the unbeliever. I'm reminded of a time when Ann Marie and I were celebrating one of our wedding anniversaries, and some friends celebrated that moment by giving us a bottle of wine. Well, we're not drinkers and I politely told them, *"thanks, but we cannot accept that gift."* You see, sometimes Satan will use people, even those who are close to you, such as family and friends to try to get you off course.

In Matthew 16:23, Peter loved Jesus so much that he didn't want him to go to the cross. Even though Peter meant well, Jesus knew that Satan had inspired his heart, and he turned to Peter and said in Matthew 16:24, *"Get thee behind me Satan."* Yes, it seemed innocent, but what if we had taken the gift, and later on Satan started putting thoughts in my mind, *"this is a special day; it's ok for you and your wife to have a drink to celebrate these wonderful years you have spent together,"* and then he will throw in his most popular line of all times, *"nobody would ever know"* and the next thing you know, we both wake up with hang-overs, all because we accepted a gift from Satan.

The Lord desires that his people be trained and empowered by His Spirit to discern and walk in Spiritual Discernment. It is not God's will that we be ignorant of the Satan's devices. The Lord desires his people to learn how to use the weapons that he has given to us so that we can demolish the enemy's strongholds in our lives. Satan knows his time is short, and our defenses must be built up in order to protect us from his attacks.

The Bible warns us in Matthew 24:24 that *"the very elect can be deceived"* if they are not careful. We can defeat Satan, but we must learn the ways of God, which means we must think with wisdom. In order to do so, our hearts must be pure so that we may see God and gain discernment. This combination of Spiritual Discernment and Divine Guidance is the source of all Spiritual Victory.

Rememeber Delilah was a *"gift"* that was given to Samson by the Philistines which were his enemy! She was on a mission of the termination of Samson. In other words, he was setup by Satan.

The gift appealed to his fleshly appetite. Delilah was used by Satan as a seducer to find out where Samson's strength came from. She seduced him, deceived him, and eventually turned him over to the enemy for his destruction.

Be very cautious of the *"gift"* Satan is attempting to give you. It can be money, power, prestige; it can be a position; it can be drugs; it can be sex; as a matter of fact, it can be whatever Satan needs it to be in order to cause your destruction. The gift may come wrapped in a beautiful package; it can be a man or a woman, but the body of Christ must have discernment and be able to determine beyond the natural, and beyond the flesh, into the realm of the Spirit.

We as people of God should be able to discern who is giving the package and why it is being given. The church today must be very careful in dealing with Satan. We must not allow Satan to overcome us by appeasing our flesh. We must be able to discern by the Spirit, what he is up to and learn how to quickly stand against his destructive ploys.

Here's an important fact about Delilah that I need to share with you, and that is that Delilah didn't come on her own, but she was sent. Delilah was sent to Samson as a "gift" with the same aspiration and intention to kill him. Five Philistine lords came to her and gave her about $8000.00 for the sole-purpose to destroy Samson.

> Judges 16:5
> *"And the lords of the Philistines came up unto her, and said unto her, Entice him, and see wherein his great strength lieth, and by what means we may prevail against him, that we may bind him to afflict him; and we will give thee every one of us eleven hundred pieces of silver."*

Here's a group of men who wanted to destroy the man of God. Even though he got caught up in many different situations, he was, in fact, still a man of God. The man whom God chose to deliver the children of Israel out of the hands of the Philistines. He was the promise of the Angel of the Lord to his mother. Yes, Samson was a man of God in a natural and spiritual battle.

The Philistines made every attempt to destroy him, but failed constantly. He was causing havoc in their kingdom and vowed to destroy them for what they had done to him and destroy everything that was not like God. His purpose was to deliver the children of Israel, and for 20 years, he could do just that, so these men conspired against him to kill him, and their weapon of choice was a *"gift"* named Delilah.

Understand people of God that there is a conspiracy to destroy you. Satan never just sent the *"Delilah gift"* into your life, but she is sent into your life at a precise time in your life for a specific purpose in your life.

Your *"Delilah gift"* is the manifestation of a particular, intentionally spiritual plan by an adversary who is utterly determined to destroy you before you are able to reach that level that God has destined for you. She is sent to assassinate those that have the potential of tearing the kingdom of the devil down. For some she may come in the form of a cigarette, for someone else she may come in the form of an alcoholic beverage, for someone else she may be crack cocaine. For someone else she may be a job, a house, or a car. She may come in many different forms, but she is a *"gift"* and her mission is to terminate you.

So many times people try to play games with Satan thinking it's some kind of game saying, *"Oh it's okay if I just do it this onetime"* but what they fail to understand is that Satan is not playing a game. The Bible says in Revelation 12:12 *"...Woe to the inhabiters of the earth, and of the sea for the devil is come down unto you, having great wrath because he knoweth that he hath but a short time."*

Satan knows his time is short, and he is not going to waste his time playing games. Listen! Once Satan sees what we have, he will then devise a way to take it from us. So it is imperative to know that Satan never gives something for anything, he always wants something in return and as Christians, we must not be quick to give in to Satan.

We must not be so ignorant as to allow Satan to come in and see all our sources of strength. The devil will not offer you something that you wouldn't want to have. If you have never had a problem with alcohol, then he will not use alcohol to try to terminate you because he knows that it will not affect you. However, he has a specially made *"gift"* that is perfectly tailored just for you just like he did for Samson.

In this spiritual warfare, there are weapons that have been formed against you that are being sent to you to penetrate your heart and for their purpose is to kill, steal and destroy. Samson kept playing around with the devil. That is why the word of God warns us in 2 Corinthians 6:17 *"Come out from among them and be ye separate saith the Lord."*

Satan has a *"gift"* with your name on it that he wants to send and penetrate your heart and destroy you with. The Bible in Ephesians 6:11 *"Put on the whole armour of God, that ye may be able to stand against the wiles of the devil."*

The gift from Satan penetrated his heart, then the Philistines bound him and the first thing they did was to take away his eye sight, why? Because Satan understands Proverbs 29:18 *"Where there is no vision, the people perish"* Satan wants to take your vision. Please do not let that *"gift"* sent from Satan take your vision.

When you lose your vision, you end up on a downward spiral into the depths of sin. It's a terrible thing to lose your vision. Samson lost his vision and was placed in fetters and made to be a grinder in the prison. You may be wounded and you may have even lost your vision, but you're not dead yet. Just pray to God that you be empowered by His Spirit to discern and walk in Spiritual Discernment.

Chapter 5

"Learning to Stand Against Satan's Attacks of the Mind"

THE WORD CARNALITY MEAN TO have the nature and characteristics of the flesh or more simply put, it means *"fleshly"* Ephesians 2:3 *"Among whom also we all had our conversation in times past in the lusts of our flesh, fulfilling the desires of the flesh and of the mind; and were by nature the children of wrath, even as others."*

Now based on this meaning of the word flesh, to be carnal means to be characterized by things that belong to the world. Paul had been talking about two kinds of people in the world: Those who are unsaved and those who are saved. All of humanity can be divided into one of these same two groups: Natural and Spiritual.

The Natural Man is a person who does not know Christ. This person does not see the importance of going to church. They don't see the importance of giving their time, their talents, nor their tithe to God. It is very difficult to get the Natural Man to be Christ-like when they don't even believe. The Natural Man does not see the need to give to the church nor does he understand why the position of the pastor should be reverenced.

> 1 Timothy 5:17
> *"Let the elders who rule well be considered worthy of double honor, especially those who labor in preaching and teaching."*

The second man Paul deals with is the Spiritual Man. The Spiritual Man is where we all are striving to be. The Spiritual Man sees things as Christ would see them and have a better understanding. The Natural cannot properly judge each situation because he/she has no Spiritual knowledge. In other words, the Natural Man would get even while the Spiritual Man would forgive.

> 1 Corinthians 3:1
> *"And I, brethren, could not speak unto you as unto spiritual, but as unto carnal, even as unto babes in Christ."*

Paul says within the camp of those who are saved, there are also two groups: Those who are mature, which he calls Spiritual and those who are immature, which he refers to as Carnal.

The Corinthian Christians who should be spiritual were Carnal and because of this, they were not able to understand the things of God. The fact that there were among them people who were filled with envy, strife, hatred, and division was proof that they were carnal minded.

All saved people have God as a permanent resident in their lives, but not nearly all have understood and/or obeyed the biblical instructions. Only until you really love and obey God with your whole heart will you move from Carnal to Spiritual. The word of God says in St. John 14:15 *"If ye love me, keep my commandments."*

The Apostle Paul, the man whom God used to write this letter uses the word *"brethren"* but if you notice, not one time does he call unsaved people *"brethren."* There are times when God is speaking directly to his people, the people who are called saints.

> 2 Chronicles 7:14
> *"If my people, which are called by my name, shall humble themselves, and pray, and seek my face, and turn from their wicked ways; then will I hear from heaven, and will forgive their sin, and will heal their land."*

In 1st Corinthians 3:1, the people receiving this letter are addressed to as *"brethren,"* which let us know that this letter is addressed to those who are sanctified in Christ Jesus. They were truly saved, but still allowing the old nature to control them. Which leads to questions like why is it that churches are not growing? Why is that we are seeing immorality and all manners of unethical misbehavior as common within the membership of the church, as we see on the outside? There can only be two answers: Unsaved church members and carnal Christians.

Carnal minded Christians think and act on a fleshly level, rather than a spiritual level. In other words, these people think and act according to their own natural senses. They walk by sight and not by faith. They make decisions not according to the word of God, but according to how they feel and it's not difficult to determine a believer's spiritual maturity or immaturity, if you discover what they feed on or the kind of nourishment they enjoy.

1st Corinthians 3:5-9

5 Who then is Paul, and who is Apollos, but ministers by whom ye believed, even as the Lord gave to every man?

6 I have planted, Apollos watered; but God gave the increase.

7 So then neither is he that planteth any thing, neither he that watereth; but God that giveth the increase.

8 Now he that planteth and he that watereth are one: and every man shall receive his own reward according to his own labour.

9 For we are labourers together with God: ye are God's husbandry, ye are God's building.

In 1st Corinthians 3:5-9, the church is pictured as a field that ought to bear fruit. The task of the ministry is the sowing of the seed, the cultivating of the soil, the watering of the plants, and the harvesting of the fruit. While we as man can be used to plant and cultivate things, only God can make things grow. Let me explain. You see, at the point of salvation; a new Christian is hypothetical a baby Christian. Paul referred to them as *"Babes in Christ"* or as we might say, *"Spiritual Babies."*

Childhood at the appropriate time is one of the most beautiful things in the world, but childhood continued to long can lead to a life misery and grief. Childhood continued to long can be a sign that something is not right. In other words, it's a sign of disorder. This is the same thing that Paul is stating. Just like a physical baby, when the spiritual baby doesn't grow, it becomes a real problem. Paul started his ministry and church in Corinth in A.D. 50. He wrote this letter from Ephesus in A.D. 56. Paul says, *"By this time, you should be young men, but you are still babes in Christ."*

Christians who are more mature need to understand these things because it helps us realize that when a person fails, it doesn't necessarily mean that they're not saved, it may mean that they are just a baby Christian. Even though they may have been saved for a long time, they still need the proper nurturing to help them grow.

Galatians 6:1-2
¹Brethren, if a man be overtaken in a fault, ye which are spiritual, restore such an one in the spirit of meekness; considering thyself, lest thou also be tempted.

²Bear ye one another's burdens, and so fulfil the law of Christ.

These Christians in Corinth, just like so many Christians everywhere, were not babies because they had not had time to grow, but they were babies because they were carnal minded. They were carnal because they had not learned to operate according to the word of God. Christians are not carnal because they have not received the word of God. It is not that they haven't heard it, because they have.

1 Corinthians 3:2
"I have fed you with milk, and not with meat: for hitherto ye were not able to bear it, neither yet now are ye able."

These believers were fed with the milk of the word of God, but the problem is that they are not doers of the word that they are hearing. The Bible says in James 1:22 *"But be ye doers of the word, and not hearers only, deceiving your own selves."*

If the believers are hearers of the word and not doers of the word, in reality, they are like the physical baby who throws his milk right back up. They did not receive it into their hearts because to receive the word of God, is to apply the word of God to your life and apply your life to the word of God.

> 1 Corinthians 3:3
> *"For ye are yet carnal: for whereas there is among you envying, and strife, and divisions, are ye not carnal, and walk as men?"*

> 1 Corinthians 3:4
> *"For while one saith, I am of Paul; and another, I am of Apollos; are ye not carnal?"*

Paul first charges them and then he asks a question. *"Are ye not carnal?"* Paul says, *"You act like other men; you are not acting like heavenly renewed men who live in the power and love of the Holy Spirit."*

When men give way to their tempers, pride, envy, and division, and they listen to people saying unkind things about others, and when a man cannot open his heart to a brother who has done him wrong and forgive him, when a woman can speak about her neighbor with contempt or have strong feelings of dislike for someone, are all the works of the carnal spirit.

Every bit of unlovingness is nothing, but the flesh. The flesh is selfish and proud and unloving; therefore, every sin against love is nothing but proof that the man is carnal. Some may say, *"I have tried to conquer it, but I cannot,"* but you cannot bear spiritual fruit while you are in the carnal state, you must have the Holy Spirit in order to love, then will you be able to conquer carnality because God will give you the Spirit to walk in love.

It's so important to study the Word of God. When you're still a spiritual baby, you need to attend Sunday school, Bible studies, men/women ministries, and other studies from time to time. The Bible says in Hebrews 10:25 *"Not forsaking the assembling of ourselves together, as the manner of some is; but exhorting one another: and so much the more, as ye see the day approaching."* We are to love one another, pray for one another, and bear one another's burdens. We are to extend hospitality to one another; we are to forgive one another, and the list goes on and on. Christian fellowship is tremendously important and as your fellowship grows deeper and stronger, you become more involved in groups within the church. There are many opportunities to exercise your gift, and there are opportunities to serve, and it will help with your growth.

Chapter 6

"Learning to Worship God in the Midst of Satan's Attacks"

WEBSTER'S DICTIONARY DEFINES THE WORD crisis as; "*a stage in a sequence of events at which the trend of all future events is determined.*"

In this life that we got, we go through all kinds of situations. We have good times and bad times.

When we are faced with a crisis in life, what do we do and how do we respond to it? One of the ways we can respond to the crisis is by "*worshiping God.*" Job is a perfect example for us. Job worshiped God in the time of crisis.

> Exodus 4:27-31
> *²⁷And the LORD said to Aaron, Go into the wilderness to meet Moses. And he went, and met him in the mount of God, and kissed him.*

28 And Moses told Aaron all the words of the LORD who had sent him, and all the signs which he had commanded him.

29 And Moses and Aaron went and gathered together all the elders of the children of Israel:

30 And Aaron spake all the words which the LORD had spoken unto Moses, and did the signs in the sight of the people.

31 And the people believed: and when they heard that the LORD had visited the children of Israel, and that he had looked upon their affliction, then they bowed their heads and worshiped.

Notice what it says in Exodus 4:31, *"And they believed."* When they heard that the LORD was concerned about them and had seen their misery, they bowed down and worshiped. In the scripture, the Israelites were in bondage and in great misery under the rule of Pharaoh in Egypt. In the midst of their crisis, they discovered that the Lord was concerned about them. The immediate response by the Israelites was that they worshiped God.

Today maybe you are going through some crisis in your life, and the Lord is telling you that he is concerned about you. Will you worship God in the midst of your crisis? When we worship God in crisis, we show forth our trust and faith in God.

Philippians 4:6-7
"Be careful for nothing; but in everything by prayer and supplication with thanksgiving let your requests be made known unto God."

"And the peace of God, which passeth all understanding, shall keep your hearts and minds through Christ Jesus."

In God's presence, we find peace, joy, and rest. God words say in Matthew 11:25 *"Come to me, all you who labor and are heavy laden, and I will give you rest."*

When Jehoshaphat faced crisis in his life when the enemy surrounded him and his people, he chose to come before God and worshiped Him. Jerusalem bowed before the LORD, worshiping the LORD.

2 Chronicles 20:18
"And Jehoshaphat bowed his head with his face to the ground: and all Judah and the inhabitants of Jerusalem fell before the Lord, worshipping the Lord."

The Bible tells us in Psalm 34:3 to *"magnify"* the Lord and not our problems. *"O magnify the Lord with me, And let us exalt his name together."* God has given us emotions and when we are struck with a crisis in our life, our emotions can get stirred up towards frustration, anger, depression, etc.... At that time, we need to direct our emotions towards God. We need to come before God worshipping Him and magnifying Him. And when I say worship, I mean giving God real praise. Understand; *"emotion without devotion is nothing more than commotion."*

"God is our refuge and strength, a very present help in trouble."
Psalm 46:1

God is our refuge, In other words; God is a safe place; God is a safety zone, and God is a shelter from danger. I know I have had storms in my life; I've had some troubled times in my life; I've had some times where

35

it seemed like I wasn't going to make it, but I'm glad that I had a refuge; I'm glad that I had a place of shelter, so my advice to you is when trouble comes your way, just remember that God is our Protector!

Not only is the Lord our refuge, but he's our refuge and our strength. The word and is a conjunction word that connects two or more phrases together, so to get the proper implication of what the writer is trying to say, you've got to connect it together!

God is our refuge AND our strength! The Lord gives us refuge in order to get us ready for the battle, how does he do that? By implanting us with His strength, so we'll be able to stand against the attacks of Satan!

God is our refuge; God is our strength, but most of all; the scripture lets us know he is also our help, as a matter of fact; he's not just our help, but it also says, *"He's a very present help in trouble."* The word present affirms to us the fact that we serve a right now God. It means that the Lord's help is immediately available to us whenever we are in trouble!

God is not a God, who did wonderful things in the past, but can do nothing now, nor is he a God, who will do great things in the future, but can do nothing now. My God is a Present Tense God! He can walk right on the scene of our lives and cause a change right now! There has been times in my life where I had been in some tight places. Yes, I have been in some trouble and didn't know what I was going to do but my God stepped in the nick of time, and that's when I found out he is my Refuge, My Strength, and Very Present Help in the time of trouble. All I had to do is trust him to do what he said he would do. God is able to show up right in the middle of all the situations in our lives, and he will make everything all right because God is our Protector! We also need to remember that God is our Provider.

Philippians 4:19
"But my God shall supply all your need according to his riches in glory by Christ Jesus."

We so many times depend on outside resources to satisfy. Things like money, prestige, activity, and amusements. All of these things can be cut off and lost in your life, but the good news from is that even if you lost everything on the outside, Health, Money, Prestige, you still have The Holy Spirit and all you have got to do is tap into the source. God is Our Protector; God is Our Provider, and if you're going to have Confidence In The Midst Of a Crisis, you have to remember that God is the Proven One.

In order for us to stand against the attacks of Satan, we need to Reflect on His Power.

"Come; behold the works of the LORD, what desolations, he hath made in the earth."

"He maketh wars to cease unto the end of the earth; he breaketh the bow, and cutteth the spear in sunder; he burneth the chariot in the fire."
Psalms 48:8-9

The scriptures say, *"Come, behold the works of the Lord."* In other words, reflect on how God has given you victory in the past, reflect on how He's brought you out in times of storm, when you were in trouble, and you didn't think you would make it through, but God turned your situation around. God hasn't brought you this far to leave you.

Remember when Satan brings his attacks against you, all you've got to do is reflect on His Power, and he'll begin to revive your spirit and rejuvenate your will to go on, and as a result, you can say what Paul said:

> *"I can do all things through Christ, who strengthens me..."*
> Philippians 4:13

Visit Our Website
divinefavorministrieschurch.org

Write to:

KDR MINISTRIES
16923 Frazho Rd.
Roseville, Michigan 48066

To place orders online, visit

www.divinefavorchurch@yahoo.com